DAILY DEVOTIONS

by Gerard Kalan

SUNSHINE MOUNTAIN PRODUCTIONS, INC.
Derry, New Hampshire
1-800-998-GLOW (4569)

for Margaret Mary Nix

Daily Devotions
©1996, Sunshine Mountain Productions, Inc., 55 Crystal Ave, Suite 248, Derry NH 03038.

ISBN 1-890017-01-9

Printed in Canada.

JANUARY 1

The Lord seeth not as man seeth, for man looketh on the outward appearance, but the Lord looketh on the heart.
    1 SAM. 16-7

Be not vain about your appearance for it is what is in your heart that matters. Understand, as the Lord does, that what you look like is not the Lord's measure of what you are.

JANUARY 2

Nothing shall be impossible unto you.
    JESUS
    MATT. 17:20

Believe in the word of Jesus that you can do anything you set out to do.

JANUARY 3

Do to me according to that which hath proceeded out of thy mouth.
   JUDG. 11:36

Do you speak the words of truth and do you suit your actions in honesty and candor to those words? Being truthful shall set you free.

JANUARY 4

Seest a man diligent in his business? He shall stand before kings.
   PROV. 22:29

Do your best and be honorable in your dealings: The reward shall come to you.

JANUARY 5

I can do all things through Christ which strengtheneth me.
  PHIL. 4:13

To love Christ is to give yourself an inner strength which will help you to solve all problems and defeat all obstacles.

JANUARY 6

Naked came I out of my mother's womb, and naked shall I return thither.
  JOB 1:21

No matter how many worldly goods we may accumulate, the eyes of the Lord see only us and our deeds. Our possessions are not what we are.

JANUARY 7

Though I be absent in the flesh, yet am I with you in the spirit.
   COL. 2:5

Feel the presence of the Lord always there in your heart to comfort and guide you.

JANUARY 8

He that is without sin among you, let him first cast a stone.
   JESUS
   JOHN 8:7

Before you pass judgment on somebody else, think about your own behavior. Are you without blemish?

JANUARY 9

I have fought a good fight. I have finished my course. I have kept the faith.
　　2 TIM. 4:7

In any job, no matter how challenging, stay to the end, finish the mission. Believe that you can do it, and you will be able to.

JANUARY 10

Acquaint now thyself with Him, and be at peace: Thereby good shall come unto thee.
　　JOB 22:21

Believe in the Lord, keep your faith in him close to your heart, and things in your own life will follow a good course.

JANUARY 11

To the weak, became I as weak, that I might gain the weak.
    1 COR. 9:22

In love and caring we must remember to deal gently with those who are weaker than we, for by sharing with them, we gain our own faith.

JANUARY 12

That which is crooked cannot be made straight: and that which is wanting cannot be numbered.
    ECCL. 1:15

Travel in the path of righteousness for a wrong turn cannot lead you to the right place. If your deeds are empty of goodness, your life will be empty of meaning.

JANUARY 13

The Son of Man came not to be ministered unto, but to minister, and to give his life as a ransom for many.

JESUS
MATT. 20:28, MARK 10:45

We must live our lives remembering the great sacrifice Jesus made for us. We must strive to make ourselves worthy of his deed.

JANUARY 14

Give and it shall be given unto you.

JESUS
LUKE 6:34

Every act of giving enriches the giver. Be generous with those less fortunate than you, and give generously of your worth.

JANUARY 15

Give instruction to a wise man, and he will be yet wiser: trench a just man and he will increase in learning.
PROV. 9:9

Be open to new ideas, new learning; for the more you learn, the wiser you will be. Be just and wise, and as the years go by, your learning and wisdom will increase.

JANUARY 16

Set your affections on things above, not on things on the earth.
COR. 3:2

The greatest rewards on earth come from faith and spirit. Enrich your soul and do not put your focus on material goods.

JANUARY 17

Whosoever is angry with his brother without a cause shall be in danger of the judgment.
> JESUS
> MATT 5:22

Any time you are angry examine your anger and understand it. If it arose from jealousy or another unworthy cause, you shall be the one to suffer.

JANUARY 18

The Lord reigneth; let the earth rejoice.
> Ps. 97:1

The Lord shall be with us and guide us each day.
It shall be a wonderful year

JANUARY 19

Hatred stirreth up strifes, but love covereth all sins.
    PROV.10:12

Try to reason away any hatred, for all it accomplishes is to make more trouble. Love brings forgiveness and peace in your own heart.

JANUARY 20

Whosoever shall call on the name of the Lord shall be saved.
    ACTS 2:21

The Lord is always there for you, and with your faith in him you will be able to surmount all difficulties that impede your path.

JANUARY 21

There is nothing unclean of itself, but to him that esteemeth any thing to be unclean, to him, it is unclean.
    ROM. 14:14

Keep your thoughts pure and unsullied, for when your mind embraces nasty thoughts, you yourself become soiled and unclean.

JANUARY 22

Let not arrogancy come out of your mouth: for the Lord is a God of knowledge, and by Him actions are weighed.
    1 SAM. 2:3

Do not be proud and over bearing to others . The Lord will judge you by what you do and how you act , not by the volume or arrogance of your voice.

JANUARY 23

Call upon Me in the day of trouble. I will deliver thee, and thou shalt glorify Me.
Ps. 50:15

The Lord is always there for you, caring and loving. In times of trouble, pay homage to him and he will be there to shelter and guide you.

JANUARY 24

Who is like thee, O Lord, among the gods? who is like Thee, glorious in holiness, fearful in praises, doing wonders?
Ex. 15:15

We can only marvel at the wonder of the Lord and glory at the light he sheds on our lives.

JANUARY 25

If you forsake the Lord, and serve strange gods, then He will turn and do you hurt.
JOS. 24:20

There is only one true God and we must worship him and not be turned aside by strange fads or attracted or odd cults with empty promises. Stay faithful to the Lord and love alone that God forever.

JANUARY 26

A time to be born, a time to die; a time to plant and a time to pluck up that which is planted.
ECCL. 3:2

Go with the flow of the cycle of life. Enjoy each phase of your life as it reveals itself to you, and know that for each season of ire there is a special meaning just for you.

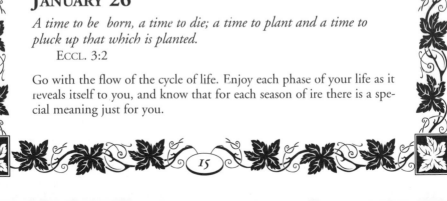

JANUARY 27

You shall walk in all the ways which the Lord your God hath commanded you, that ye may live and that it may be well with you.
> DEUT. 5:33

Follow the words and commands of God in your daily life and your faith will help you to achieve serenity and richness in all you do.

JANUARY 28

My thoughts are not your thoughts, neither are your ways My ways , saith the Lord.
> ISA. 55:8

Your neighbor will not see things the way you see them, but you are not right and he is not wrong. You may just be different. Respect his ways as you would want him to respect yours.

JANUARY 29

Peace be unto thee, and peace be to thy helpers; for thy God helpeth thee.
    1 CHR. 12:18

Live peacefully along with your family and friends for your are never alone. God is always there besides you to help and comfort you.

JANUARY 30

I have learned, in whatsoever state I am, therewith to be content.
    PHIL. 4:11

You have a role to play in the scheme of things, and whatever it may be, no one else can play that role as well as you.

JANUARY 31

Surely Goodness and mercy shall follow me all the days of my life:
And I will dwell in the house of the Lord for ever
  Ps. 23:6

If you have lived a righteous life, following the commands of the Lord,
your life will be blessed and the Lord will be with you for all your time
unto eternity.

🍃 🍃 🍃

FEBRUARY 1

Bless them that curse you, do good to them that hate you.
> JESUS
> MATT 5:44

Only by love and kindness can we conquer the hatred and evil that lies in some people's hearts. Do not let the rage of others infect your own spirit.

FEBRUARY 2

Heaven and earth shall pass away, but my words shall not pass away.
> JESUS
> MATT 24:35 MARK 13:31 LUKE 21:33

The words of Jesus are eternal, and while you may lose everything else in your world, the precepts that He has laid down to govern man's behavior shall prevail forever.

FEBRUARY 3

The steps of a good man are ordered by the Lord; and he delighteth in his way.
    Ps. 37:23

When you behave in a righteous way, not only does it enrich your own spirit but the Lord delights in your virtue.

FEBRUARY 4

When thou makest a feast, call the poor, the maimed, the lame, the blind: And thou shall be blessed, for they cannot recompense thee.
    JESUS
    LUKE 14:13-14

When you give to charity or in other ways help those less fortunate than yourself you cannot expect any material reward, but the reward shall be in the Lord's blessing; for by giving to others you enrich your own soul.

FEBRUARY 5

When a man's ways please the Lord, he maketh even his enemies to be at peace with him.
> PROV. 16:7

If you walk in the ways of the Lord and do his biding, your behavior will even affect those who wish you ill and turn their evil thoughts aside from harming you.

FEBRUARY 6

O Daniel, servant of the living God, is thy God whom thou servest continually able to deliver thee?
> DAN. 6:20

Have the faith that if you walk with Him and look to Him and expect Him to help you, He will never fail you.

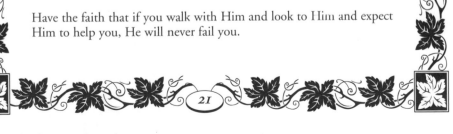

FEBRUARY 7

Put off all these: anger, wrath, malice, blasphemy, filthy communication out of your mouth.
    COL. 3:8

Keep the words that come out of your mouth clean and pure; for ugly and wrathful language will, in the end, turn against you and corrupt your own thoughts.

FEBRUARY 8

Let us, who are of the day, be sober, putting on the breastplate of faith and love, and for an helmet, the hope of salvation.
    1 THESS. 5:8

Protect your heart with faith in God's Holy Ordinances and the love of Jesus Christ. Let your mind be filled with thoughts of God's plan for salvation.

FEBRUARY 9

Sorrow is better than laughter: for by the sadness of the countenance the heart is made better.
ECCL. 7:3

Sometimes we can not understand the sadness of life, and we sin to laughter. But sorrow makes us more introspective and slows us down to look into our own motives and actions.

FEBRUARY 10

Thou shalt find Him, if thou seek Him with all thy heart and with all thy soul.
DEUT. 4:29

If sometimes your faith wavers and you do not feel His presence, turn all your thoughts and all your actions to seeking Him, and you will find that He is there for you.

FEBRUARY 11

But the dove found no rest for the sole of her foot, and she returned unto him ... And the dove came in to him in the evening; and lo, in her mouth was an olive leave.

GEN. 8:9-11

God's will is that we wait until he has prepared our resting place. Patience is a virtue.

FEBRUARY 12

What doth the Lord require of thee, but to do justly, and to love mercy, and to walk humbly with God?

MIC. 6:8

The Lord is not demanding, and if in your daily life, you do those things that you know are right, you will be walking in his path to find inner peace.

FEBRUARY 13

God is in the midst of her; she shall not be moved: God shall help her, and that right early.
   Ps. 46:5

When our faith is shaken; when others doubt and try to move us, God is on our side. To be strong in the house of God one would gladly endure all the enemies against us.

FEBRUARY 14

Confidence in an unfaithful man in time of trouble is like a broken tooth, and foot out of joint.
   Prov. 25:19

Chose those whom you would trust wisely, for hasty, choices may be unwise and then when you depend on someone, he or she may not be there for you.

FEBRUARY 15

Did ever people hear the voice of God speaking out of the midst of the fire, as thou hast heard, and live?
> DEUT. 4:33

No matter how great your trouble, take comfort in the fact that God is there beside you, speaking out to you, and you shall triumph over that which besets you, for in his voice you will find strength.

FEBRUARY 16

Thou shall lend unto many nations, but thou shalt not borrow.
> DEUT. 15:6

To be a debtor is to limit your freedom of action. Be generous and giving, but careful when you obligate yourself to others.

FEBRUARY 17

He turned the sea into dry land: They went through the flood on foot; there did we rejoice in him.
> Ps. 66:6

Is it not true that sometimes in the very time of distress and sadness one can be able as never before to rejoice in the Lord?

FEBRUARY 18

A gift doth blind the eyes of the wise, and pervert the words of the righteous.
> Deut. 16:19

Be careful about accepting gifts, for although some are given in the fullness of heart, others may be otherwise motivated. Think well before accepting such tokens.

FEBRUARY 19

If we walk in the light, as He is in the light, we have fellowship one with another.
   1 JOHN 1:7

We can be brothers to all mankind if we follow the path of goodness and virtue led by our Lord.

FEBRUARY 20

When I was a child, I spoke as a child. I understood as a child, I thought as a child; but when I became a man, I put away childish things.
   1 COR. 13:11

Sometimes it is tempting to revert to childish ways and behave without regard to long-term consequences. But when you become an adult you know that your life has meaning and there are rules to live by and one must abide by them.

FEBRUARY 21

He that hideth hatred with lying lips, and he that uttereth a slander, is a fool.

PROV. 10:18

Know that when you lie or defame another person, it just demonstrates your own ignorance. The wise man has no need of such devices and only the fools stoop to lies and deceit.

FEBRUARY 22

He that believeth not is condemned, already, because he hath not believed in the name of the only begotten Son of God

JESUS
JOHN 3:18

Without belief, your soul will be lost, for there is no salvation except through accepting Jesus, the Son of God.

FEBRUARY 23

Dearly beloved, avenge not yourself.
ROM. 12:19

There are times when to take no action, to let events pass, takes immeasurably higher strength than to act. One must learn when to exercise restraint.

FEBRUARY 24

All the rivers run into the sea; yet the sea is not full.
ECCL. 1:7

There is no limit to the compassion of our Lord. It is boundless and deep like the ocean and all the troubles and sorrows in the human life can never fill the depth of his loving.

FEBRUARY 25

If thy right hand offend thee, cut it off and cast it from thee.
> JESUS
> MATT 7:1

If there are things or people in our lives that we know are not good for us, we must have the strength to rid ourselves of them without looking back or regretting.

FEBRUARY 26

Let the heavens rejoice, and let the earth be glad: let the sea roar, and the fullness thereof.
> PS. 96:11

When God is in your heart, the joy of believing can make you feel as if the earth joins with you in the celebration of faith.

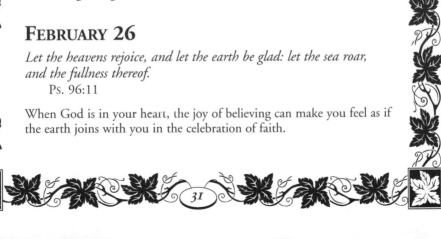

FEBRUARY 27

Grace be with all them that love our Lord Jesus Christ in sincerity.
EPH. 6:24

To love the Lord Jesus Christ is to fill your life with lightness and grace. This love will enlighten every deed and make rich all your days.

FEBRUARY 28

Fret not, thyself.
Ps. 37:1

When worries beset you, remember that God has a thousand ways to show you his love and help. Just trust and you will know his will.

MARCH 1

A time to keep silence and a time to speak,
  EC.3:7

There are times when you want to rush forth in a gush of words, but
think first; for sometimes silence speaks more eloquently than words.

MARCH 2

The blood of Jesus Christ, His Son, cleanseth us from all sin.
  1 JOHN 1:7

We must live our lives remembering the great sacrifice Jesus made for
us. Let our own lives be a beacon of goodness as we follow his words.
It is through His Blood our sins are "washed away."

MARCH 3

*Have faith that whatever you ask for in prayer is already granted you,
and you will find that it will be.*
MARK 11:24

We may not realize it at the time, but prayers are heard and answered.
You may not recognize the answers at the time, but believe in the power
of prayer and it will accomplish miracles.

MARCH 4

Let us eat and drink; for tomorrow we shall die.
ISA 22:13. 1

Live richly with pleasure for the well of life is not limitless. Make every
minute of your life count knowing that each one is precious. God has
not promised you tomorrow.

MARCH 5

He that speaketh of himself seeketh his own glory.
> JESUS
> JOHN 7:18

Curb idle boasting for, in the end, it can only diminish your own image. Let your actions, not your words, show the measure of your goodness.

MARCH 6

Nothing shall be impossible unto you.
> MATT. 17:20

We may do whatever we wish, for Christ has enabled us to do what we will. With faith, all accomplishment, become possible.

MARCH 7

Boast not thyself of tomorrow; for thou knowest not what a day may bring forth.
  PROV. 27:1

Live each day to the glory of God for events are unpredictable and each day will be a fresh page in the book of your life.

MARCH 8

The race is not to the swift, not the battle to the strong, neither yet bread to the wise nor yet riches to men of understanding, nor yet favour to men of skill; but time and chance happeneth to them all.
  ECCL. 9:11

Even though all the odds seem to be in one's favor, it does not necessarily mean success, for many other random factors affect events. To keep the faith is the most important element in influencing events in your life.

MARCH 9

I am the bread of life: he that cometh to me shall never hunger, and he that believeth in me shall never thirst.

> JESUS
> JOHN 6:35

The deepest hunger of all is the hunger for spiritual peace. Believing in our Lord will nourish the soul and fulfill all hungers.

MARCH 10

He that loveth not his brother whom he hath seen, how can he love God whom he hath not seen?

> 1 JOHN 4:20

Cultivate love in your heart for your fellow man. If you are unable to love those with whom you deal in your life, you will not be able to love God who is not visible to you.

MARCH 11

But without faith it is impossible to please Him: For he that cometh to God must believe that He is, and that He is a rewarder of them that diligently seek Him.
HEB. 11:6

Empty promises and protestations mean nothing without the true belief and faith that prompts them. With this faith you will seek God and you will find rewards.

MARCH 12

Rest in the Lord and wait patiently for Him.
PS. 37:7

Learn patience, for it takes away worry. The Lord said He would come and His Promise is equal to His presence.

MARCH 13

Be ready in the morning, and come up...present thyself there to me in the top of the mountain. And no man shall come up with thee.
EX. 34:2-3

Start each day with a few quiet minutes alone; a time to feel the presence of God in your heart.

MARCH 14

Let not mercy and truth forsake thee: Bind them about thy neck.
PROV. 3:3

Those things that make us good are an integral part of our being. Never subvert your instincts toward charity and truth for they are the very essence of a good person. Take a strong hold to those good things.

MARCH 15

Come unto me, all ye that labour and are heavy laden, and I will give you rest.
> JESUS
> MATT. 11:28

Turn to Jesus with your problems and worries, for He is able to bear them, to even fix them, and give you rest.

MARCH 16

Thou shalt not harden they heart, nor shut thine hand from thy poor brother.
> DEUT. 15:7

Do not judge a person by his worldly worth, for his true worth cannot be measureD in what he possesses. Rather, keep your heart open and welcoming to those who are less fortunate and have not acquired worldly goods.

MARCH 17

One man esteemeth one day above another: another esteemeth every day alike. Let every man be fully persuaded in his own mind.
ROM. 14:5

You write your own life story, and it is in your power only to judge the worth of each of your actions. Do not be swayed by another's evaluation, for your life is your own unique property.

MARCH 18

Comfort ye, comfort ye my people saith your God.
ISA. 40:1

When God comforts us, it is not to make us comfortable, but to make us comforters of others.

MARCH 19

He that spareth his rod hateth his son: but he that loveth him chasteneth him betimes.
PROV. 13:24

It is often hard to punish and be severe, but love and caring has many faces. Sometimes it is necessary to show ones love by being harsh against transgression.

MARCH 20

And the spirit cried, and rent him sore, and came out of him.
MARK 9:26

Evil never gives up its hold without a fight. We never pass into our spiritual heritage readily, but through a grim struggle.

MARCH 21

Behold, I set before you this day a blessing and a curse. A blessing if ye obey the commandment of the Lord your God, which I command you this day. And a curse, if ye will not obey.
   DEUT. 11:26-28

The Lord is always with you in his goodness, but live your life righteously for He will know when you step from His path, and He will withdraw His blessings from you.

MARCH 22

We are made partakers of Christ, if we hold the beginning of our confidence steadfast unto the end.
   HEB. 3:14

God's pattern is not always immediately apparent. It takes patience, but we will get great things from God if we are able to hold on to the end.

MARCH 23

Thy money perish with thee, because thou hast thought that the gift of God may be purchased with money.
ACTS. 8:20

In the end, everything material you have acquired is as nothing, for you cannot take it with you. But if you have lived your life in God's way and been righteous, this then you shall take with you into the kingdom of heaven. Do not try to purchase righteousness.

MARCH 24

Ye shall not go out with haste.
ISA. 52:12

We rush around in our modern lives always in a hurry. Stop a minute. Ask God to go before you, to make the way easy, to bless you to be a blessing.

MARCH 25

Beloved, do not be surprised at the ordeal that has come to test you...you are sharing what Christ suffered: so rejoice in it.
      1 PETER 4:12

To wait for God and to suffer His will is to be close to Him in sharing His suffering. When we are tested, we can feel the pain Jesus felt and be enriched by sharing His agony.

MARCH 26

Lo, I am with you all the appointed days.
      MATT. 28:20

Even when you do not feel his presence, He is there for you. Have belief in the faithfulness of God. In Him you surely will prevail.

MARCH 27

When thou passest through the waters, I will be with thee; and through the rivers, they shall not overflow thee; when thou walkest through the fire, thou shalt not be burned.
ISA. 43:2

When God is at your side, you are made stronger and invulnerable. Troubles will come and sorrow and grieving will be your lot, as it is all peoples', but with your faith in the Lord you will survive them.

MARCH 28

For I reckon that the sufferings at this present time are not worthy to be compared with the glory which shall be revealed in us.
ROM. 8:18

Do not think your suffering is in vain, for we are made perfect and brought to our own glory through tribulation.

MARCH 29

And when forty years were expired, there appeared to him in the wilderness of mount Sinai an angel of the Lord in a flame of fire.
  ACTS. 7:30

God has unlimited time and is never in a hurry. Sometimes we must wait for a long time for a desired end to be achieved, but we must remember the patience of the Lord and bide our time in peaceful waiting.

MARCH 30

Thou shalt keep the commandments of the Lord thy God, to walk in His ways and to fear Him.
  DEUT. 8:6

The ten commandments are the rules the Lord has proclaimed for us to live by, and let them be your guide in all your actions, for by obeying them, you will be blessed.

MARCH 31

What doth the Lord thy God require of thee, but to fear the Lord thy God, to walk in all His ways, and to love Him, and to serve the Lord thy God with all thy heart and with all thy soul.
DEUT. 10:12

If you walk in the ways of the Lord and, even in the darkest moments, believe in His ways and dedicate your heart to loving Him, your life will have meaning and your soul will have peace.

APRIL 1

Walk worthy of the vocation wherewith ye are called.
  EPH. 4:1

No matter what the work you do, whether you like it or have been forced to do it due to circumstances, do your job the best you can, and your accomplishment, great or small, will fill you with great pride.

APRIL 2

The testimony of the Lord is sure, making wise the simple.
  PS. 19:7

To believe in the Lord and to follow his teachings will bring a wisdom that far surpasses any learning you may acquire elsewhere. His word embodies the richest wisdom man can achieve.

APRIL 3

I do not count the sufferings of our present life worthy of mention when compared with the glory that is to be revealed and bestowed upon us.
ROM. 8:18

In times of trial and suffering, you must cling to the faith that this is but a preparation and that some day He will come for you and you shall rejoice, for in heaven, we will not be bothered by earthly problems again.

APRIL 4

Ye are all children of light and the children of the day.
1 THESS. 5:5

The love of Christ for his children is boundless, and in His grace your life shall be made meaningful and rich.

APRIL 5

Come now and let us reason together, saith the Lord.
    ISA. 1:18

Do not become involved in an argument with angry words, but calmly sit down with your opponent and make peace. Then in a quiet fashion, face the problem, for in this way useless anger can be defused and ugly disagreements resolved.

APRIL 6

Render therefore unto Caesar the things which are Caesar's and unto God the things that are God's.

    JESUS
    MATT. 22:21, MARK 12:17, LUKE 20:25

Perform your material concerns always with awareness that ultimately homage to God is paramount.

APRIL 7

Though he slay me, yet will I trust in him.
    JOB 13:15

You must keep your faith in the Lord no matter how cruel life seems, and come what may, you must hold fast to your confidence in God's faithfulness.

APRIL 8

God that made the world and all things therein, seeing that He is Lord of heaven and earth, dwelleth not in temples made with hands.
    ACTS. 17:24

Although you may worship God in temples and churches, feel His presence in all places of our world. God exists everywhere from the smallest flower to the sparkling stars of the universe; He is with us everywhere.

APRIL 9

Blessed is the man that walketh not in the counsel of the ungodly, nor standeth in the way of sinners, nor sitteth in the seat of the scornful.
   Ps. 1:1

Be aware of those who transgress God's commandments, for seeking their counsel and company will corrupt you. Seek those with goodness in their hearts with whom you can share God's grace.

APRIL 10

All things work together for good to them that love God.
   Rom. 8:28

There are many strands in life, and sometimes they may seem to be going in opposite directions. But for those with faith, the strands interweave each with the other so that in the end they form a beautiful pattern of life, honoring God.

APRIL 11

Thou shalt not harden thy heart nor shut thy hand from thy poor brother.
  DEUT. 15:7

All men who are of good faith are equal in the eyes of the Lord, and we must follow His example and cherish people for what they are, not what they have.

APRIL 12

If a man know not how to rule his own house, how shall he take care of the church of God?
  1 TIM. 3:5

Living by the commandments and keeping order in your own life and house is as important as tending to your church, for each action we take impacts on every other action, and disorder in one place breeds disorder in the other.

APRIL 13

And Jesus, being full of the Holy Ghost, returned from Jordan, and was led by the Spirit into the wilderness, being forty-five days tempted of the devil.
> LUKE 4:1-2

Temptation often besets a man with its strongest power when he is nearest to God.

APRIL 14

The Lord is merciful and gracious, slow to anger, and plenteous in mercy.
> PS. 103:8

If we model our behavior after that of the Lord, such behavior is its own reward, and we will be beloved and respected by all.

APRIL 15

The word is very nigh unto thee, in thy mouth, and in thy heart.
DEUT. 30:14

Faith rests on the naked Word of God. When we take Him at His Word, our heart is at peace.

APRIL 16

Come unto me, all ye that labour and are heavy laden, and I will give you rest.
JESUS
MATT. 11:28

In the love of Jesus we will find refreshment for our souls.

APRIL 17

I have heard thy prayer, I have seen thy tears; behold, I will add unto thy days fifteen years.
    ISA 38:5

Prayer has the force to change our lives. God is there, hearing our prayers and acting on them in His mercy.

APRIL 18

Give me neither poverty nor riches; feed me with food convenient for me.
    PROV. 30:8

Be content with that which meets your basic needs so that you are not driven to illness from hunger or lack of shelter, but do not lust for more than your life requires.

APRIL 19

Thou shalt love the Lord thy God with all thy heart, and with all thy soul, and with all thy mind. This is the first and great commandment.
>   JESUS
>   MATT. 22:37-38

Whoever you are, whatever you do, in your heart and mind you must carry the love for the Lord thy God at all times and in all places.

APRIL 20

The Lord that delivered me out of the paw of the lion, and out of the paw of the bear, He will deliver me out of the hand of this Philistine.
>   DAVID
>   1 SAM 17:37

When the odds seem overwhelming, trust in the Lord and He will come to your rescue.

APRIL 21

Yea, though I walk through the valley of the shadow of death, I will fear no evil for Thou are with me.
　　Ps. 23:4

Even in the shadow of death, have no fear, for you are not alone. The Lord is there to give you strength and courage at a time of trial.

APRIL 22

I even reckon all things as pure loss because of the priceless privilege of knowing Christ Jesus my Lord.
　　Phil. 3:8

Do not reckon the cost of an action when the results are worthy. We cannot be of great use to others without cost to ourselves.

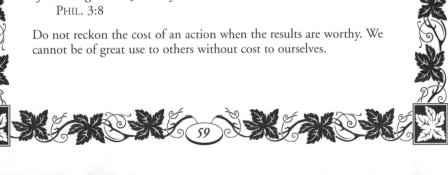

APRIL 23

Thou knowest all the wickedness which thine heart is privy to.
     1 KINGS 2:44

Look deeply into yourself and know yourself, both the bad and the good, for who amongst us does not have some unworthiness. Through recognizing our own wickedness, we can control it and cast it from our minds.

APRIL 24

A new commandment I give unto you, That ye love one another.
     JESUS
     JOHN 13:34

Embrace your fellow man as you would have him love you.

APRIL 25

His mischief shall return upon his own head.
Ps. 7:16

All our actions have consequences, and although it may not be immediate, sooner or later you will regret doing something that you know is not right, for it will return to plague you.

APRIL 26

A man is not justified by the works of the law, but by the faith of Jesus Christ.
GAL. 2:16

There is a law that is higher even than the law of the land, and man must ultimately be judged by that higher law.

APRIL 27

*And it shall come to pass that whosoever shall call on the name of the
Lord shall be delivered.*

JOEL 2:32

It is vain to look for deliverance anywhere else; but with God you will
find it, for here you have His royal will to make it sure.

APRIL 28

*Keep yourselves from the accursed thing, lest ye make yourselves
accursed.*

JOSH. 6:18

Be wary of the company you keep, for if you consort with evil, that evil
will, in the end, corrupt your own behavior.

APRIL 29

All the law is fulfilled in one word, even in this: Thou shalt love thy neighbor as thyself.
GAL. 5:14

No person is more valuable than any other, nor more invulnerable to hurts and slights. Govern your actions by how you would feel if such a deed were done to you. All of the commandments are reckoned with this one act.

APRIL 30

Stand still and see the salvation of the Lord.
Ex. 14:13

If your spirit does not feel willing, do not force yourself to any action. Wait with patience until all is clear and do not go against the healing of the Lord.

❦ ❦ ❦

MAY 1

As I was with Moses, so I will be with thee.
GOD TO JOSHUA.
JOSH. 1:5 JOSH. 3:7

God may not make his presence known, but He is there with you at all times, in trouble and in happiness. Just as you see God manifested in others, He can do the same for you.

MAY 2

This is His commandment, That we should believe on the name of His Son Jesus Christ, and love one another.
1 JOHN 3:23

It is God's will that we revere his son, Jesus Christ, and that in our dealings with others, we have love in our hearts.

MAY 3

He maketh sore, and bindeth up: He woundeth and His hands make whole.
   JOB 5:18

We must have faith that life's hard moments, when sorrows befall, are but another expression of God's will, and through our faith in that will, our sorrows will be healed.

MAY 4

Except ye utter by the tongue words easy to be understood, how shall it be known what is spoken? For ye shall speak into the air.
   1 COR. 14:9

Do not cloak your speech in abstract, undecipherable language, for clarity of mind is reflected in your speech.

MAY 5

I beseech Thee, O Lord, take away the iniquity of Thy servant; for I have done very foolishly.
2 SAM 24:10

We make mistakes, but God is merciful and He will listen to our plea for forgiveness. Recognize the error of your ways, and pray that your sins may be forgiven.

MAY 6

We went through fire and water: But thou broughtest us out into a wealthy place.
PS. 66:12

As contradictory as it may seem, only that man is at rest who attains it through the challlenge of conflict.

MAY 7

Two are better than one; because they have a good reward for their labour.
ECCL. 4:9

When faced with a difficult task, if it is possible to find a willing partner, the task will seem lighter, for working in harmony with another brings its own special rewards to the spirit.

MAY 8

Evil communications corrupt good manners.
1 COR. 15:33

Look well upon all communication, for if it is with flaw and error, and if in intent it is evil, in itself it will corrupt both he who sends it and he who receives it.

MAY 9

All things are possible to him that believeth.
     MARK 9:23

No goal is too lofty, no dream is too impossible, no victory too unobtainable to one who follows the Lord's word and, in his heart, cherishes and believes in Him.

MAY 10

In the beginning God created the heaven and the earth.
     GEN. 1:1

There is nothing without God, for he is the creator of the universe and all that exists within it. Be humble in your worship of the Almighty.

MAY 11

Woe to him that is alone when he falleth; for he hath not another to help him up.
ECCL. 4:10

If you love not and travel through life in a lonely way, when troubles beset you, then you will find no one to care or help. Then will you know the coldness of despair in the lonely place you have chosen.

MAY 12

To obey is better than sacfifice, and to hearken than the fat of rams.
1 SAM. 15:22

Instant obedience is the only kind of obedience, for delay and procrastination is disobedience. We rob God along with robbing ourselves and others when we put off doing something we know must be done.

MAY 13

Ye cannot drink the cup of the Lord, and the cup of devils.
1 COR. 10:21

There is no such thing as a "little corruption." Once you have stooped to an evil deed, even if it be considered insignificant by you, you have sinned in the eyes of God.

MAY 14

Woe unto him that buildeth his house by unrighteousnes, and his chambers by wrong.
JER. 22:13

If a structure that looks magnificent has termites in the cellar, it will one day collapse. So it is if a structure is built on an evil deed; in the end it will be destroyed by its own unworthiness.

MAY 15

Shall I refuse to drink the cup of sorrow which the Father hath given me to drink?
   JOHN 18:11

Open your heart to pain, and it will do you more good than if you were full of feeling and devoutness, for it is through suffering that we grow. Jesus is asking "shall I go aginst God's will and not suffer as He desires?"

MAY 16

The Lord is the strength of my life: Of whom shall I be afraid?
   Ps. 27:1

Face every trouble that may beset you with courage and fearlessness, for the belief in the Lord is like armour that shields you and keeps you from harm.

MAY 17

At their wit's end, then they cry unto the Lord in their trouble and He bringeth them out.
   Ps. 107:27-28

Do not get discouraged; keep your faith in the Lord and it may be that most unexpectedly, the troubles you face become resolved.

MAY 18

If we confess our sins, He is faithful and just to forgive us our sins.
   1 JOHN 1:9

We must be aware if we transgress, but the Lord in his mercy will forgive us if we recognize our sins and truly repent.

MAY 19

Be of good courage, and He shall strengthen your heart, all ye that hope in the Lord.
    Ps. 31:24

Keep your courage up, believe in the Lord, and through that belief, you will become stronger and more able to face adversity.

MAY 20

For Sarah conceived and bare Abraham, a son in his old age, at the set time of which God had spoken to him.
    GEN. 21:2

Our timetables mean nothing, for God has His set times. It is not for us to know them; we must wait for them, and we will not be disappointed.

MAY 21

Let him that thinketh he standeth take heed lest he fall.
   1 COR. 10:12

Be not overly proud in your position in life, for nothing is fixed except our faith in the Lord. Even the strongest may be brought low one day.

MAY 22

For I was hungered, and ye gave me meat: I was thirsty, and ye gave me drink: I was a stranger, and ye took me in: Naked and ye clothed me: I was sick and ye visited me: I was in prison, and ye came unto me.
   JESUS
   MATT. 25:35-36

Scorn not the poor and ragged, for Jesus himself has known this fate, and the loving kindness that eased his path should be an example for all men to govern their own behavior toward the homeless and downtrodden.

MAY 23

For Abraham, when hope was gone, hoped on in faith. His faith never quailed.
ROM. 4:18-19

Even when things seem the blackest, hold on to your faith, for faith will help you to survive the blackest times that confront you.

MAY 24

God hath not given us the spirit of fear; but of power, and of love, and of a sound mind.
2 TIM. 1:7

We are empowered with so many gifts from the day we are born. Cherish and appreciate your legacy, and through your faith, enrich these gifts with love and kindness.

MAY 25

Faithful are the wounds of a friend; but the kisses of an enemy are deceitful.
     PROV. 27:6

Look beyond honeyed words to the deeds, for the true friend will prove himself by his caring deeds, and the enemy may speak kindly while stabbing you in the back.

MAY 26

The Lord is my helper, and I will not fear what man shall do unto me.
     HEB. 12:12

Belief in the Lord will make you strong against any indignities that other men may impose on you, so live fearlessly, secure that your faith will shelter you from enemies.

MAY 27

For every child of God overcomes the world, and the victorious principle which has overcome the world is our faith.
    1 JOHN 5:4

Faith can help solve any situation, no matter how dark it may seem to be. A quick lifting of the heart to God in a moment of real faith in Him will quickly help you to find an answer to your problem.

MAY 28

He spake and it was done; He commanded, and it stood fast.
    PS. 33:9

Never underestimate the power of the Lord, for He who created the universe is everywhere amongst us at all times.

MAY 29

Where envying and strife is, there is confusion and every evil work.
JAMES 3:16

Envy is an ugly emotion that destroys contentment and spoils the joys of our own existence. Glory in the gifts that you have been given and do not lust after the goods of others.

MAY 30

Defile not therefore the land which ye shall inhabit.
NUM. 33:34

This world, which is the Lord's creation, is therefore sacred, and as we revere him, we must revere this beautiful universe we have been blessed with and treat it with respect and reverence.

MAY 31

Herein do I exercise myself, to have always a conscience void of offense toward God, and toward men.
ACTS 24:16

To live with a free conscience is a great blessing, for knowing that you walk in God's path of righteousness enriches you and all those you love.

❧ ❧ ❧

JUNE 1

Fear ye not the reproach of men, neither be you afraid of their revilings.
ISA. 51:7

If you are righteous in your actions, the Lord will know and the reproaches of others do not matter, for in your heart you will be strong in the knowledge that you have done the right thing.

JUNE 2

He that soweth to his flesh shall of the flesh reap corruption, but he that soweth to the Spirit shall of the Sprit reap life everlasting.
GAL. 6:8

If you are governed by lustful appetites, in the end you will be destroyed, but if you are governed by your spiritual life, in the end you will be rewarded.

JUNE 3

Wherefore lift up the hands which hang down, and the feeble knees;
and make straight paths for your feet, lest that which is lame be
turned out of the way; but let it rather be healed.

HEB. 12:12-13

Pay as little attention to discouragement as possible. Keep your eye on
your goal, and forge ahead in spite of all obstacles.

JUNE 4

The merciful man doeth good to his own soul; but he that is cruel
troubleth his own flesh.

PROV. 11:17

Kindness and compassion to others will enrich you, but if you are cruel,
you will pay the price, for your cruelty will, in the end, turn against
your own soul.

JUNE 5

I have learned in whatsoever state I am, therewith to be content.
    PHIL. 4:11

Learn to make the most of your life whatever your situation may be, for every day is a precious gift. Use it well.

JUNE 6

He that goeth forth and weepeth, bearing precious seed, shall doubtless come again with rejoicing, bringing the sheaves with him.
    Ps. 126:6

When we take an active part in bringing joy to another, even if while sorrowing, mourning a personal loss, there will come a time when we will reap a reward in happiness from that deed.

JUNE 7

Thine ears shall hear a word behind thee, saying,
This is the way, walk ye in it, when ye turn to the right hand, and
when ye turn to the left.
> ISA. 30:21

Are you confused about which path you should follow in your life?
Turn to God and His Will shall make your way clear.

JUNE 8

Whosoever shall compel thee to go a mile, go with him twain.
> JESUS
> MATT. 5:41

Always strive for even more than you are asked for; your efforts will be
noted and rewarded.

JUNE 9

The Lord is a God of knowledge, and by him actions are weighed.
    1 SAM 2:3

His eye is always upon you, and fair judgment will be made of your deeds. Walk in the path of righteousness and fear not that judgment.

JUNE 10

The Lord hath sent strength for thee.
    PS. 68:35

The Lord imparts to us that basic strength of character which makes everything in our lives work with intensity and decision. And the strength is continuous; reserves of power come to us which we can not exhaust.

JUNE 11

How are the mighty fallen, and the weapons of war perished!
2 SAM. 1:27

No man reaches such a high estate that he may not be reduced to a sorry state. Be not proud, for no man's status is secure except as he has faith in the Lord.

JUNE 12

When thou goest, thy way shall be opened up before thee step by step.
PROV. 4:12

If you find barriers in your path of duty, believe in the Lord and keep moving. And with faith, you will find that you will cross through all barriers to achieve your aims.

JUNE 13

He raiseth up the poor out of the dust, and lifteth up the beggar from the dunghill.
   1 SAM 2:8

The Lord is all-powerful and it is His will that can empower the weak and enrich the poor.

JUNE 14

Be strong in the Lord and in the power of His might.
   EPH. 6:10

Know that the Lord is with you at all times and fear not, for he is strong, and if you have faith, He will be there with you to shield and protect you from harm.

JUNE 15

Do violence to no man, neither accuse any falsely.
LUKE 3:14

Be kindly in your deeds and truthful in your words, for violence and falsehood will, in the end, damage your own soul.

JUNE 16

If thy right eye offend thee, pluck it out and cast it from thee; for it is profitable for thee that one of thy members should perish, and not that thy whole body should be cast unto hell.
JESUS
MATT 5:29

If you have an evil thought, or if one you associate with is evil, get rid of that thought and cast that person from you, for in that way you save yourself from contamination of your own spiritual purity.

JUNE 17

I will call on the Lord who is worthy to be praised; so shall I be saved from mine enemies.

> 2 SAM 22:4
> Ps. 18:3

Your faith in the Lord is an armor against your enemies. Believe in Him, and He will keep you safe.

JUNE 18

I have chosen thee in the furnace of affliction.

> Is. 48:10

Fear not, Jesus is with thee in all thy fiery trials. In his presence is both comfort and safety. He will never desert you.,

JUNE 19

I sought the Lord and He heard me, and delivered me from all my fears.
    Ps. 34:4

You must seek the Lord and He will answer, and through your belief in Him, you will be made strong and able to cope with adversity with courage.

JUNE 20

Judge not and ye shall not be judged: condemn not, and ye shall not be condemned.
    LUKE 6:37

Who but the Lord is qualified to judge his fellow; who is so wise; who is so just? Only the Lord can make such judgments in His infinite wisdom.

JUNE 21

He that is of a perverse heart shall be despised.
PROV. 12:8

Keep your heart clear and honest, for perversity will be recognized and you shall lose the love of man and be a pariah amongst others.

JUNE 22

I called him, but he gave me no answer.
S. OF S. 5:6

If you think a prayer has gone unanswered, you are wrong. No prayer is lost, and no prayer is unnoticed by God. Some that we count as refusals or denials are simply delays. Be patient: God hears you.

JUNE 23

He shall have judgment without mercy, that hath showed no mercy.
    JAMES 2:13

How you behave toward others will determine how they behave toward
you. If you show no mercy, you will be treated without regard or kindness.

JUNE 24

*A merry heart doeth good like a medicine: but a broken spirit drieth
the bone.*
    PROV. 17:22

Laughter refreshes the soul and is a balm to the body. With faith, your
spirits can be light and your heart happy.

JUNE 25

He hath acquainted Himself with my beaten path. When He hath searched me out, I shall come out shining.
     JOB 23:10

The path full of sorrow and joy, of suffering and healing balm, of tears and smiles, of trials and victories will be lit by the love of Him who watches over us.

JUNE 26

Lord, Thou art God, which hast made heaven, and earth, and the sea.
     ACTS 4:24

Feel the power of the Lord, for he who has created everything is all-knowing, all-wise, and your life is safe in His hands.

JUNE 27

As a consuming fire, He shall destroy them, and He shall bring them down before thy face.
DEUT. 9:3

Never doubt the power of the Lord and that those who transgress will feel His wrath for He is almighty and all-knowing.

JUNE 28

And therefore will the Lord wait that he may be gracious unto you...blessed are all they that wait for him.
ISA.30:18

God knows when the time is right and we are spiritually ready to receive the blessing to our profit and to His glory,

JUNE 29

Prepare your hearts unto the Lord, and serve Him only.
     1 SAM. 7:3

Do not be beguiled by false cults promising easy access to Heaven and blessings. There is only one Lord, and he does not absolve one of pain and suffering, but faith in him will help you to prevail and be rewarded.

JUNE 30

And Jesus lifted up his eyes and said, Father, I thank thee that thou hast heard me.
     JOHN 11:41

God hears our prayers and is pleased by them. The answers may be a long time in coming, but God has his own timetable and we must abide by it.

JULY 1

If thou seek him, He will be found of thee.
1 CHRON. 28:9

The Lord's will might not always be apparent in your life, but through faith and prayer, you shall find him there with you at all times to comfort and heal.

JULY 2

Wide is the gate and broad is the way that leadeth to destruction.
JESUS
MATT. 7:13

Your path is beset with temptations and seductions. You must always keep on the straight and narrow, for to wander off is to court your own destruction.

JULY 3

Awake, O north wind; and come, thou south, blow upon my garden, that the spices thereof may flow out.
S. OF S. 4:16

The richness of a Christian life is the many diverse breezes that flow through it, for through our actions in the many acts of our life based on our faith, we create beauty.

JULY 4

Whither thou goest, I will go; and where thou lodges, I will lodge: thy people shall be my people, and thy God my God.
RUTH 1:16

Where love exists, commitment must exist, even if it involves sacrifice, for without commitment, love is empty and meaningless.

JULY 5

If thy foot offend thee cut it off: It is better for thee to enter halt into life, than having two feet be cast into hell.

> JESUS
> MARK 9:45; MATT. 18:8

Do not compromise with your beliefs, even if admitting a mistaken course of action causes pain and loss. It is better to have a clear conscience than to suffer the ill ease of guilty knowledge.

JULY 6

Although the fig tree shall not blossom, neither shall fruit be in the vines...Yet I will rejoice in the Lord, I will joy in the God of my salvation.

> HAB. 3:17,18

In the times of distress, turn to God. In the midst of trouble indulge in the sacred joy of God and know that there will be salvation from Him.

JULY 7

Fear the Lord and serve Him in truth with all your heart.
1 SAM. 12:24

Do not hold back anything in your love of the Lord in your faith, but fill your heart and soul with your undying devotion.

JULY 8

If you believe not his writings, how shall ye believe my words?
JESUS
JOHN 5:47

Know your Bible, study and learn it, for there you will find the truth, and by understanding the words, become wise.

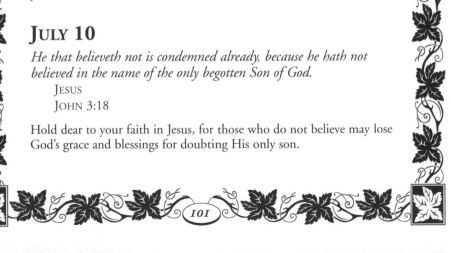

JULY 9

Whereby are given unto us exceeding great and precious promises.
2 PETER 1:4

Use God's promises as an everyday source of comfort, for God does not deny His word and He will not say no to something He has promised.

JULY 10

He that believeth not is condemned already, because he hath not believed in the name of the only begotten Son of God.
JESUS
JOHN 3:18

Hold dear to your faith in Jesus, for those who do not believe may lose God's grace and blessings for doubting His only son.

JULY 11

Seek the Lord and his strength: Seek his face evermore.
    Ps. 104

Let your life be a quest for the Lord, for He is there always with you. You must only lift your eyes above the tasks of daily living to see the face of God.

JULY 12

I send you forth as sheep in the midst of wolves: Be ye therefore wise as serpents, and harmless as doves.
    JESUS
    MATT. 10:16

Our faith in God does not keep us from dangerous situations and challenges, but if you meet them with God's wisdom and keep your own nature pure and gentle, that will deflect danger more surely than rage.

JULY 13

Thou couldest have no power at all against me, except it were given thee from above.
JOHN 19:11

There is no power possible unless it has been God's will to grant it. Nothing that is not God's will can come into the life of one who trusts in God.

JULY 14

When I looked for good, then evil came unto me: and when I waited for light, there came darkness.
JOB 30:26

We do not always understand God's ways, and sometimes when life is darkest, our faith may be shaken. But hold firm, for in the end, we will come to understand that everything has a reason and a purpose.

JULY 15

Behold, how great a matter a little fire kindleth.
JAMES 3:5

A small action that seems insignificant, a word spoken in haste that seems unimportant may trigger off an undesired chain of events. Do not act thoughtlessly in haste lest you cause a spark that grows into a dangerous flame.

JULY 16

Ye have built houses of hewn stone, but ye shall not dwell in them: Ye have planted pleasant vineyards, but ye shall not drink wine of them.
AMOS 5:11

God is a jealous God. To forget Him is to put all of your efforts in jeopardy.

JULY 17

We must through much tribulations enter in the kingdom of God.
  ACTS 14:22

The sweetest joys in life are the fruits of sorrow. We seem to need suffering to help us to appreciate the joys of blessing.

JULY 18

Wheresoever the carcase is, there will the eagles be gathered together.
  JESUS
  MATT. 24:28

Be not a predator like those who gather like birds of prey in times of trouble to see what profit they can make of another's tragedy.

JULY 19

Beware of false prophets, which come to you in sheep's clothing, but inwardly they are ravening wolves.
>JESUS
>MATT. 7:15

These cult leaders may come to you with honeyed tongues promising great rewards and glories with little effort, but beware, for their promises are empty and their words deceitful.

JULY 20

I believe God that it shall be even as it was told me.
>ACTS. 27:25

Let us keep our love simple and take God at His word so our lives may be all sunshine in the sweetness of our Lord.

JULY 21

Except ye repent, ye shall all likewise perish.
> JESUS
> LUKE 13:3

Each of us may make a mistake and do something we know is not right, but by recognizing our wrong and repenting we are saved.

JULY 22

He that spareth his rod hateth his son; but he that loveth him chasteneth him betimes.
> PROV. 13:24

It is easier to ignore bad behavior on the part of others and be indifferent, but where there is love, there is responsibility. Sometimes we must do or say things we dislike because of our love for another.

JULY 23

And Jacob was left alone, and there wrestled a man with him until the breaking of the day.
GEN. 32:24

If you must fight all night, pray all night. Do not give up, but continue until you get your blessing from the Lord.

JULY 24

We brought nothing into this world and it is certain we can carry nothing out.
1 TIM. 6:7

Do not sacrifice your soul to acquire material things, for in the end, goods are as nothing, but our spiritual soul lives forever.

JULY 25

He that worketh deceit shall not dwell within my house.
　　Ps. 101:7

The Lord is all-knowing and all-seeing, and if you practice deceit He will know and cast you from Him.

JULY 26

And the rest, some on boards, some on broken pieces of the ship. And so it came to pass that they escaped all safe to land.
　　ACTS 27:44

Follow God's word when in a crisis, and you shall arrive safely in port.

JULY 27

Ye are like unto whited sepulchers, which indeed appear beautiful outward.
> JESUS
> MATT. 23:27

Do not trust outward appearances, for a face may be beautiful, but look behind it to the nature of the person. It may be that a lovely face hides an ugly soul.

JULY 28

As a man chasteneth his son, so the Lord thy God chasteneth thee.
> DEUT. 8:5

We are all God's children and when we take a misstep He rebukes us as He would His own Son.

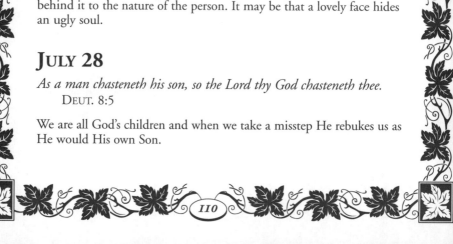

JULY 29

They that go down to the sea in ships that do business on great waters; these see the works of the Lord, and His wonders in the deep.
   Ps. 107:23-24

Sometimes in the bustle of busy lives and crowded cities, we lose sight of God, but in the solitude of nature's wonders, sea, mountains, desert, we can feel the very presence of God and sense Him near us.

JULY 30

Better is a little with righteousness than great revenues without right.
   Prov. 16:8

Do not be dazzled by great wealth dishonestly acquired, for a modest portion earned honestly has more worth in the eyes of God.

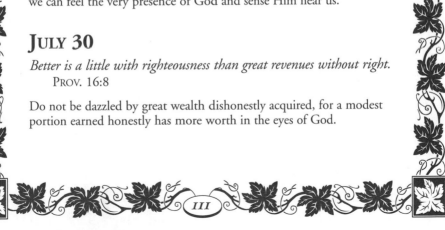

JULY 31

The grass withereth, the flower fadeth: But the word of our God shall stand forever.
    Isa.40:8

The word of God is eternal and shall survive when all else may perish.

AUGUST 1

Woe unto them that seek deep to hide their counsel from the Lord.
   ISA. 29:15

The Lord is all-seeing and all-wise, and we cannot mask evil intents or actions from Him no matter how well we conceal them, for He can understand our motives and aims.

AUGUST 2

Let no man deceive you with vain words.
   EPH. 5:6

Do not let flattery playing upon your vanity block out the real meaning of honeyed words, for they may be a mask to lead you into the wrong path.

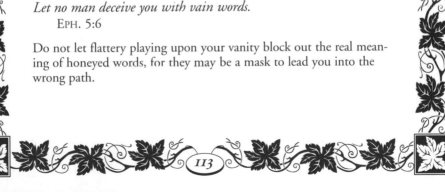

AUGUST 3

Blessed are they that have not seen, and yet have believed.
JOHN 20:29

God's will may not always be apparent, but for those who have patience and believe, He will make His word real in fact as well as in faith.

AUGUST 4

Because thou hast rejected the word of the Lord, He hath also rejected thee from being King.
1 SAM. 15:23

Do not turn away from the word of the Lord, for those things that you seek and desire will not come to you unless you hold steadfast in your faith.

AUGUST 5

Whosoever heareth these sayings of mine and doeth them, I will liken him unto a wise man, which built his house upon a rock.
> JESUS
> MATT. 7:24

Let the words of Jesus be the foundation of your life and it will be a strong and sturdy base that will support you through times of trouble and sorrow.

AUGUST 6

Cursed be he that doeth the work of the Lord deceitfully.
> JER. 48:10

Be wary of those who pretend to be the Lord's servants and would use His words to further their own goals. Look into their deeds, not their words, to see if they are truly worthy.

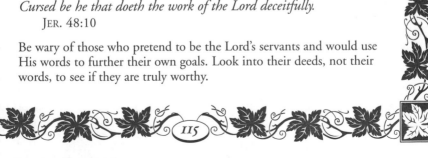

AUGUST 7

Blessed are all they that wait for Him.
    ISA. 30:18

It may take patient waiting for the moment that God is revealed to us, but in that time of waiting, we receive His blessing .

AUGUST 8

The prophet that hath a dream, let him tell a dream, and he that hath My word, let him speak My word faithfully,
    JER. 23:28

The Word of the Lord is a guide to a righteous life and by living by that Word we will find our own inner peace and contentment.

AUGUST 9

God is our refuge and strength, a very present help in trouble.
Ps. 46:1

Each life contains a full share of conflict and trouble, and sometimes we feel alone facing our problems, but God is there with us. Take comfort in His presence.

AUGUST 10

Thou has enlarged me when I was in distress.
Ps. 4:1

Though our troubles cause pain, it is through suffering that we grow in the spirit and our souls becomes enlarged

AUGUST 11

What doth the Lord require of thee, but to do justly, and to have mercy, and to walk humbly with God?
MIC. 6:8

God makes few demands upon us, but it is in the way we live with justice and mercy and faith in Him that we earn His blessings.

AUGUST 12

By their fruits ye shall know them.
JESUS
MATT. 7:20

It is not with our words or our acquisitions that we earn our worth, but by our deeds and our behavior toward other people; so shall we be recognized.

AUGUST 13

If this counsel or this work be of men, it will come to naught; But if it be of God, he cannot overthrow it.
ACTS 5:38-39

The deeds and works of men have only a temporal life, and in time, will disappear. But the works and Word of God are eternal.

AUGUST 14

The Lord will perfect that which concerneth me.
Ps. 138:8

Things do not always happen on the schedule we would have them happen on, but have patience and do not get discouraged. With trust in the Lord, you will achieve your goals.

AUGUST 15

Fools despise wisdom and instruction.
PROV. 1:7

Scorn not the advice of those who have gained wisdom, but heed them well, for each of us can learn much from others who have been there before us.

AUGUST 16

Why call ye me Lord, Lord, and do not the things which I say?
JESUS
LUKE 6:46

If you preach the word of the Lord and pretend to honor him, but live not a righteous life, you will not be deceiving the Lord, for He is all-knowing and will not be taken in by false declarations of faith.

AUGUST 17

And so after he had patiently endured, he obtained the promise.
  HEB. 6:15

God's promises cannot fail in their accomplishments. Those who wait patiently cannot be disappointed. Believing shall cause expectations to be realized.

AUGUST 18

Precept must be upon precept, precept upon precept; line upon line, line upon line: here a little, and there a little.
  ISA. 28:10

A house is not built from the roof down. You must build your good life by every small deed done in a righteous manner, for it is the small acts that build a strong foundation for the big decisions.

AUGUST 19

Whatsoever ye do in word or deed, do all in the name of the Lord Jesus.
COL. 3:17

Let every action in your life be guided by the precepts of Jesus and let Him be with you at all times.

AUGUST 20

Cast thy bread upon the waters: For thou shall find it after many days.
ECCL. 11:1

If you cast substances such as money, goods, and talents to good use, you shall receive it back in a short time. Thereafter you shall always have substance to cast rather than be someone who has nothing to offer.

AUGUST 21

It is the Lord: Let Him do what seemeth Him good.
　　1 SAM. 3:18

See God in everything, and God will make beautiful all that you see.

AUGUST 22

They have sown the wind, and they shall reap the whirlwind.
　　HOS. 8:7

An action may seem to be small or insignificant to you, but beware, for the small action may trigger a chain reaction that, in the end, becomes overwhelming.

AUGUST 23

Be ye doers of the word, and not hearers only.
      JAMES 1:22

It is not enough to listen to a sermon and then ignore the words
as you go about your daily life. Let the words govern each smallest
action and decision.

AUGUST 24

Where there is no vision, the people perish.
      PROV. 29:18

There is a deep hunger in all people that cannot be fulfilled by worldly
success. Only by faith in our Lord will you be able to satisfy this spiritual need.

AUGUST 25

Let us not love in word, neither in tongue; but in deed and in truth.
1 JOHN 3:18

We may speak words of love, but it is in our actions that we will be judged. Let them be truthful and righteous.

AUGUST 26

My speech shall distill as the dew, as the small rain upon the tender herb and as the shower upon the grass.
DEUT. 32:2

The word of God is omnipresent, nourishing all things and bringing beauty and health to all the things of nature.

AUGUST 27

Wheresoever the carcass is, there will the eagles be gathered together.
JESUS
MATT. 24:28

Be not a predator like those who gather as birds of prey in times of trouble to see what profit they can make of another's tragedy.

AUGUST 28

Said I not unto thee that, if thou wouldst believe, thou shouldest see the glory of God?
JOHN 11:40

You do not have to understand all God's ways. Some day you will see the glory of God in the things which you do not understand today.

AUGUST 29

He that cometh to me shall never hunger, and he that believeth on me shall never thirst.

> JESUS
> JOHN 6:35

Through our faith, our hunger shall be satisfied and our thirst slaked, for our Lord will care for those who believe.

AUGUST 30

Fear ye not, stand still, and see the salvation of the Lord which He will show to you today.

> EX. 14:13

Be courageous and patient, for the Lord is there with you and will guide you to salvation in His own time.

AUGUST 31

The testimony of the Lord is sure, making wise the simple.
  Ps. 19:7

To know and to follow the word of the Lord is the road to wisdom
which will make all of our lives richer and more meaningful.

❧ ❧ ❧

SEPTEMBER 1

With all thy heart, and with all thy soul, and with all thy mind.
    JESUS
    MATT. 22:37; MARK 12:29

Do not hold back in your love and belief in the Lord, but dedicate your whole spirit to your belief in Him.

SEPTEMBER 2

Dread not, neither be afraid of them. The Lord, your God, which goeth before you, He shall fight for you.
    DEUT. 1:29-30

In the many battles of life, you are not alone. God is at your side giving you courage to face your travail.

SEPTEMBER 3

And the Lord said...Satan hath desire to have you, that he may sift you as wheat, but I have prayed for thee, that thy faith fail not,.
    LUKE 22:31-32

Jesus' sacrifice on the cross gives us the victory.

SEPTEMBER 4

Do all that is in thine heart; for the Lord is with thee.
    2 SAM. 7:3

Your heart will dictate the right path when faced with hard decisions, for you are not alone. The Lord is with you in help and guidance.

SEPTEMBER 5

The good shepherd giveth his life for his sheep.
JESUS
JOHN 10:11

Jesus' love for us is like that of a guardian ready to give his life for us who live with the awareness of sheep.

SEPTEMBER 6

Be strong and courageous, be not afraid or dismayed.
CHRON. 32:7

You are not alone as you go into battle. The Lord is your ally and with Him beside you, no enemy is unconquerable.

SEPTEMBER 7

After they were come to Mysia they assayed to go into Bithnia: But the Spirit suffered them not.
    ACTS 16:7

In the kingdom of Christ there are not only times for action, but times when you must forbear acting. Use judgment and exercise patience. Before you rush into a situation, find the leading of the Spirit.

SEPTEMBER 8

Save thou us out of his hands, that all the kingdoms of the earth may know that Thou art the Lord God, even Thou only.
    2 KINGS 19:19

Worship only the one true God who is all-knowing and all-powerful. Deny those who would claim power to other Gods.

SEPTEMBER 9

Who shall separate us from the love of Christ? Shall tribulation, or distress, or persecution, or famine, or nakedness, or peril, or sword?
ROM. 8:35

We hold fast to the love of Christ as He loves us, no matter what forces conspire against us to destroy our faith in Him.

SEPTEMBER 10

Seek and ye shall find.
JESUS
MATT 7:7, LUKE 11:9

Our goals are not always easily seen or easily achieved, but do not give up. Through diligence and honest effort, you shall reach your goals.

SEPTEMBER 11

I will give myself unto prayer.
    PS. 109:4

Take the time to often be alone with God, and through prayer, you will achieve growth in holiness.

SEPTEMBER 12

Study to be quiet and do your own business.
    1 THESS. 4:11

Nothing is to be gained by unwarranted interference in the affairs of others. Focus on running your own affairs in the path of righteousness.

SEPTEMBER 13

Be not afraid of their faces, for I am with thee to deliver thee, saith the Lord.

JER. 1:8

You will never be ashamed to be a child of God. He will alway bring you through.

SEPTEMBER 14

I send you forth as sheep in the midst of wolves, be ye therefore wise as serpents, and harmless as doves.

JESUS
MATT 10:24

Life is full of perils and evil people who would do you harm. You can not defeat them with arms, but rather wisdom of God will protect you from their evil intent.

SEPTEMBER 15

Let me not be ashamed, let not mine enemies triumph over me.
Ps. 25:2

Live in a way that you may be proud of and it will give you power over your enemies. Faith in the Lord will give you power to defeat your enemies.

SEPTEMBER 16

And he took them, and went aside privately into a desert place.
Luke 9:10

The soul in one single quiet hour of prayer will often make more progress than in days in the company of others.

SEPTEMBER 17

If thine enemy be hungry give him bread to eat: and if he be thirsty give him water to drink.
PROV. 25:21

We can turn an enemy into a friend by treating him as a friend. Kindness and caring will deflect anger and turn dislike into respect.

SEPTEMBER 18

If any man serve me, him will my Father honour.
JESUS
JOHN 12:26

To believe in the words of Jesus and to live by them earns the blessings of God.

SEPTEMBER 19

Thou shalt not covet thy neighbour's house, thou shalt not covet thy neighbour's wife, nor his manservant, nor his maidservant, nor his ox, nor his ass, nor any thing that is thy neighbour's.
> Ex. 20:17

Cast envy from your heart and keep your eyes firmly on your own life, for wanting that which is not yours can only diminish your soul.

SEPTEMBER 20

He that is unjust in the least is unjust also in much.
> JESUS
> LUKE 16:10

There is no such thing as a small act of injustice. Any act of injustice is a sin, even though it may appear to be minor, for the act itself is the flaw, not the importance of it.

SEPTEMBER 21

He that walketh in darkness and hath no light, let him trust in the name of Jehovah and rely upon his God.
    Is. 50:10

We must trust God. While we trust, God can work. Worry prevents Him from doing anything for us.

SEPTEMBER 22

As many as I love, I rebuke and chasten.
    JESUS
    REV. 3:19

Righteous behavior is expected of us, and if we fail, we must submit to paying the price of chastisement because He loves us.

SEPTEMBER 23

Wrath killeth the foolish man, and envy slayeth the silly one.
JOB 5:2

The wise man harbors in his heart neither anger nor envy, for these do nothing but harm to he who exercises them.

SEPTEMBER 24

Whosoever shall keep the whole law and yet offend in one point, he is guilty of all.
JAMES 2:10

We cannot pick and choose which laws we wish to obey. Each is as important as another, and unless we obey all, we have obeyed none.

SEPTEMBER 25

By reason of breaking they purify themselves.
    JOB 41:25

God uses most for His glory those people and things which are most perfectly broken. The sacrifices He accepts are broken and contrite hearts.

SEPTEMBER 26

My doctrine is not mine, but His that sent me.
    JESUS
    JOHN 7:16

The word of Jesus comes directly from His father, God, and is to be regarded with reverence as most holy.

SEPTEMBER 27

Riches certainly make themselves wings; they fly away as an eagle toward heaven.
    PROV. 23:5

Do not build your life on acquiring material riches, for they can disappear and leave you impoverished. Rather, build your life on riches of the soul, for these will never leave you.

SEPTEMBER 28

Stand fast and hold the traditions which ye have been taught.
    2 THESS. 2:15

Do not let the stresses and tempo of modern life shake your belief. It is this belief which shall help you cope with the tensions in your life.

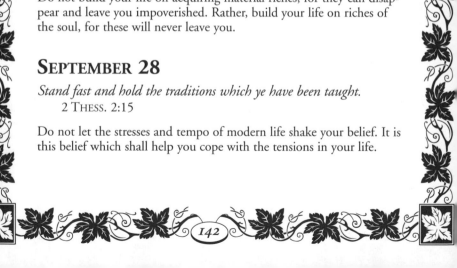

SEPTEMBER 29

Therefore will the Lord wait, that he may be gracious unto you.
ISA. 30:18

When you do not feel God's presence, do not say that He has forgotten you. He is there, perhaps tarrying a little while to make you love Him better.

SEPTEMBER 30

The rich and poor meet together; the Lord is the maker of them all.
PROV. 22

We are all the children of God and in His eyes we are all equal. Do not deem yourself better than another man because of your worldly possessions. Only in faith might you be richer.

❧ ❧ ❧

OCTOBER 1

The race is not to the swift, nor the battle to the strong, neither yet bread to the wise, nor yet riches to men of understanding, nor yet favour to men of skill; but time and chance happeneth to them all.
ECCL. 9:11

No matter what our skills or abilities are there is just so much in our lives that we can control; for random factors may have a strong influence on events. The only surety is faith in our Lord.

OCTOBER 2

He which soweth sparingly shall reap also sparingly.
2 COR. 9:6

If we do not make an effort, we cannot succeed, for there is no reward to one who does not exert himself to reach a goal.

OCTOBER 3

Let us lay aside every weight and the sin which doth so easily beset us,
and let us run with patience the race that is set before us.
HEB. 12:1

We can set our will against doubt, just as we do against any other sin,
and as we stand firm and refuse to doubt, we shall be blessed.

OCTOBER 4

Whatsoever ye do, do it heartily, as to the Lord and not unto men.
COL. 3:23

The only judgment that has any meaning is the judgment of the Lord.
Live in His path of righteousness and what men may judge matters not,
for you will get your reward in His blessings.

OCTOBER 5

And the peace of God which transcends all our powers of thought,
shall be a garrison to guard your hearts and minds in the Christ Jesus.
    PHIL. 4:7

The peace of God is that internal calm which lies deep down in your
heart secure from any external trouble or disturbance.

OCTOBER 6

If I ascend up into heaven, Thou art there: If I make my bed in hell,
behold, Thou art there.
    PS. 139:8

Our earthly life is but a passage to the next, and our early actions will
determine where we shall spend eternity. So be righteous and you shall
receive your reward, for there is no escape from God. He is everywhere.

OCTOBER 7

Rejoice with them that do rejoice, and weep with them that weep.
  ROM. 12:15

Join with your fellow men in their sorrows and joys, for through our sharing the emotions of others, we ourselves grow in spirit and love.

OCTOBER 8

For we know that if our earthly house of this tabernacle were dissolved, we have a building of God, a house not made with hands, eternal in the heavens.
  2 COR. 5:1

Our faith does not reside in earthly buildings, and if they were all to be destroyed, it would not matter, for the house we dwell in is the house of God, and it is our abode eternally.

OCTOBER 9

There is no peace, saith the Lord, unto the wicked.
ISA. 48:22

The wicked may prosper in worldly things, but their hearts are ill at ease and their heads rest uneasy in sleep, and in the end, their deeds shall betray them.

OCTOBER 10

Though I be absent in flesh, yet am I with you in the spirit.
1 COR. 5:3

We may not see the Lord or touch him, but know that He is with us at all times with love and caring.

OCTOBER 11

There hath not failed one word of all his good promise.
    1 KINGS 8:56

Trust with patience that the Lord will fulfill all his promises. Heaven shall fade and the earth shall crumble away before God's word shall fail.

OCTOBER 12

Because ye have forsaken the Lord, He hath also forsaken you.
    2 CHRON. 24:20

Even when troubles beset you and you do not feel the Lord's grace, you must keep faith in Him, for if you leave Him, He will leave you.

OCTOBER 13

Be not afraid, but speak, and hold not thy peace: For I am with thee.
    JESUS
    ACTS. 18:9-10

It takes courage sometimes to speak the truths which others do not want to hear, but even if your words are received with anger, you are not alone, for the Lord stands beside you.

OCTOBER 14

This God is our God for ever and ever. He will be our guide even unto death.
    PS. 48:14

The Lord is there for you every moment of your life; in joy and in sorrow. Forever.

OCTOBER 15

Is anything too hard for the Lord?
GEN. 18:14

When we believe in God enough and do His will, nothing is too hard for Him to do for those who trust in Him.

OCTOBER 16

The triumphing of the wicked is short, and the joy of the hypocrite but for a moment.
JOB 20:5

If you achieve your ends through unjust means, do not celebrate, for in the end, your deeds will turn upon you and your triumph will turn to ashes.

OCTOBER 17

Every man shall receive his own reward according to his own labour.
   1 COR. 3:8

Nothing can be attained by doing nothing, and he who shirks his fair share of work shall not receive his portion of gains.

OCTOBER 18

Keep thy tongue from evil, and thy lips from speaking guile.
   PS. 34:13

Evil words are the visible sign of an evil in your soul. Keep your thoughts pure and good, and your words will follow, and your purity will be blessed.

OCTOBER 19

If God be for us, who can be against us?
    ROM. 8:31

If God is on your side, there is no enemy powerful enough to hurt you, for the power of God surpasses that of any man.

OCTOBER 20

Under hopeless circumstances, he hopefully believed.
    ROM. 4:18

No matter how bleak the circumstances, no matter how impossible the solution may seem, hold fast to your faith in Him and He will lead you to the solution of the problem.

OCTOBER 21

I am come a light into the world that whosoever believeth on me should not abide in darkness.

> JESUS
> JOHN 12:46

Jesus is that light that has come to lead all from the darkess of evil and damnation.

OCTOBER 22

A wise man feareth and departeth from evil; but the fool rageth, and is confident.

> PROV. 15:26

It is not cowardly to be fearful and to flee from evil, for only a fool feels that he can conquer it, and in the end, he may himself be conquered.

OCTOBER 23

There is no difference between the Jew and the Greek for the same Lord over all is rich unto all that call upon Him.
  ROM. 10:12

The Lord does not see the difference in color, race, or creed, for there is only one God over all and He has compassion for men of all types.

OCTOBER 24

Thou who hast showed us many and sore troubles, wilt quicken to us again.
  Ps. 71:20

Never doubt God. Never say that He hast forsaken or forgotten. Never think that He is unsympathetic. Trust and He will be there for you.

OCTOBER 25

The thoughts of the wicked are an abomination to the Lord.
PROV. 15:26

All our thoughts are as an open book to the Lord, and if there dwell evil thoughts, they offend Him and turn Him away from the offender.

OCTOBER 26

If thou wilt enter into life, keep the commandments.
JESUS
MATT. 19:17

By obeying the commandments, one will enter into life, living it richly, meaningfully, and with grace.

OCTOBER 27

He that diggeth a pit shall fall into it.
ECCL. 10:8

Do not think that you can hide unjust or evil actions, for sooner or later, they will come back to trap you in their snares.

OCTOBER 28

Casting all your cares upon him; for he careth for you.
1 PETER 5:7

When the burdens of life seem too heavy to bear, remember that you are not alone. He is there beside you to uphold you with His love and caring.

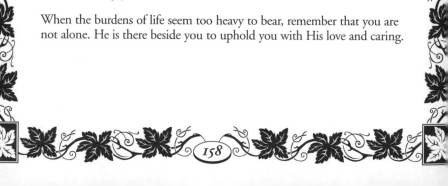

OCTOBER 29

Thou, Lord, art high above all the earth: Thou art exalted far above all Gods.
   Ps. 97:9

He is all-powerful, all-seeing, all-knowing and we honor His exalted position, knowing that He is above all other things of the earth.

OCTOBER 30

How hard it is for them that trust in riches, to enter into the Kingdom of God.
   JESUS
   MARK 10:24

If you devote your life entirely to acquiring material things, you may be rich in goods, and but you will be poor in spirit, and in your eternal life you will then be impoverished.

OCTOBER 31

Teach me thy way, O Lord, and lead me in a plain path.
  Ps. 27:11

Let yourself be directed by God; follow where He may lead and be assured it will be a path that leads to your rewards.

NOVEMBER 1

Be not righteous over much; neither make thyself over wise.
   ECCL. 7:1

Remain humble no matter how much wisdom you may acquire or how many fine deeds you may do. Your wisdom and deeds are but grains of sand when we think of our Lord, all-knowing and all-powerful.

NOVEMBER 2

Ye rich men, weep and howl for your miseries that shall come upon you.
   JAMES 5:1

If you devote life to acquiring riches and ignore or neglect your spiritual nature, your life will be empty and your riches meaningless.

NOVEMBER 3

Ye shall not see wind, neither shall ye see rain; yet that valley shall be filled with water, that ye may drink, both ye, and your cattle and your beasts.
    2 KINGS 3:16

Faith gives us the vision to expect the impossible miracle that God will cause to happen when He must to fill our needs.

NOVEMBER 4

Remember the days of old, consider the years of many generations: Ask thy father, and he will show thee, thy elders, and they will tell thee.
    DEUT. 32:7

There is much to be gained by listening to the elderly, for they have learned from many years of life and we can glean wisdom from them.

NOVEMBER 5

Pride goeth before destruction, and a haughty spirit before a fall.
    PROV. 10:18

Have not overweening pride and a patronizing attitude toward others for life situations change, and if you face failure, those around you will not comfort you, but they will rejoice that you are brought low.

NOVEMBER 6

As with the buyer, so with the seller; as with the lender, so with the borrower; as with the taker of usury, so with the giver of usury to him.
    ISA. 24:2

The way you behave toward others will influence how they treat you, and if you are not just in your dealings, others will feel free to treat you unjustly.

NOVEMBER 7

The world passeth away, and the lust thereof: But he that doeth the will of God abideth for ever.
   1 JOHN 2:17

Pledge yourself to do the will of God in your every deed, for in that way, and that way alone, will you gain the kingdom of heaven.

NOVEMBER 8

Be thou faithful unto death, and I will give thee a crown of life.
   JESUS
   REV. 2:10

Through your faith and love for Jesus will you find your life rich and full. Pay homage to Him in your every thought and deed and you will be blessed.

NOVEMBER 9

For this our light and transitory burden of suffering is achieving for us a weight of glory.
2 COR. 4:17

The moment of suffering passes, but the gift it leaves in our soul lasts forever.

NOVEMBER 10

He will not fail thee, neither forsake thee: fear not, neither be dismayed.
DEUT. 31:8

When the dark clouds hover overhead, and all seems impossible in your life, do not doubt. He is there. Be courageous in your troubles, and He will reveal Himself.

NOVEMBER 11

The Lord gave and the Lord hath taken away: blessed be the name of the Lord.
JOB. 1:21

It is not given for mere man to understand God's will, and if you feel that He has forsaken you, do not despair, but have patience. And His will shall be made clear to you.

NOVEMBER 12

Let him that is athirst come. And whosoever will, let him take the water of life freely.
REV. 22:17

The welcoming hand of the Lord is always held out to the needy, and He gives His love to those whose hearts have been starved and whose souls have been weary.

NOVEMBER 13

If thine eye be evil, thy whole body shall be full of darkness.
> JESUS
> MATT. 6:23

Look upon the world with a clear and innocent eye. Those who see only evil around shall themselves fall heir to evil thoughts.

NOVEMBER 14

Meddle not with him that flattereth with his lips.
> PROV. 10:18

Listen carefully for an inner voice when you are being flattered, for sometimes the flatterer has a motivation to befuddle your senses through your vanity.

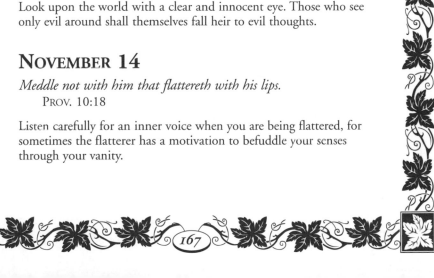

NOVEMBER 15

Many sorrows shall be to the wicked: but he that trusteth in the Lord, mercy shall compass him about.
    Ps. 32:10

The wicked by their sins stand alone and deserted, but he who has faith in the Lord shall always have the comfort and caring in times of hardship and sorrow.

NOVEMBER 16

As you share the sufferings you share the comfort also.
    2 Cor. 1:7

Do not fret and wait with anxiety for the sufferings to pass; rather get out of it all you can both for yourself and others, according to the will of God.

NOVEMBER 17

All things whatsoever ye would that men should do to you, do ye even so to them.
> JESUS
> MATT. 8:26

Do you have it ever in your mind that how you treat others is how you wish to be treated? If you follow this rule, you will never harm another as you would not wish to be harmed.

NOVEMBER 18

The love of money is the root of all evil.
> 1 TIM. 6:10

He who puts all his emotional life into the love of money will find his soul lonely and his heart bare, for money cannot love in return.

NOVEMBER 19

And there was Anna, a prophetess…which departed not from the temple, but served God with fastings and prayer night and day.
LUKE 2:36-37

By praying, we learn to pray, and the more we pray and the oftener pray, the better we pray.

NOVEMBER 20

What things soever ye desire, when ye pray, believe that ye receive them, and ye shall have them.
JESUS
MARK 11:24

Prayer backed by unswerving faith can accomplish what seem like miracles.

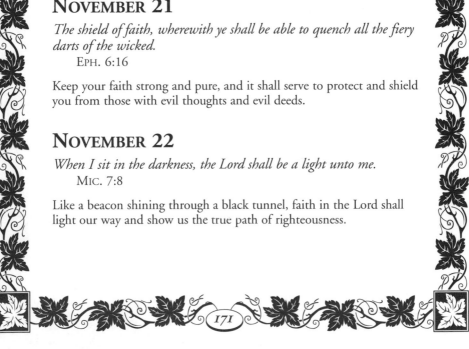

NOVEMBER 21

The shield of faith, wherewith ye shall be able to quench all the fiery darts of the wicked.
   EPH. 6:16

Keep your faith strong and pure, and it shall serve to protect and shield you from those with evil thoughts and evil deeds.

NOVEMBER 22

When I sit in the darkness, the Lord shall be a light unto me.
   MIC. 7:8

Like a beacon shining through a black tunnel, faith in the Lord shall light our way and show us the true path of righteousness.

NOVEMBER 23

They speak a vision of their own heart, and not out of the mouth of the Lord.
JER. 14:15

There are those among us who claim loyalty to other Gods and preach of newly founded creeds. Beware these false prophets for they speak falsely out of their own vanity or need for power. There is but one God.

NOVEMBER 24

Be not afraid of him, saith the Lord: for I am with you to save you.
JER. 42:11

The faithful need have no fear of any man or event for the Lord watches over them and will keep them from harm.

NOVEMBER 25

Behold, how good and how pleasant it is for brethren to dwell together in unity!
Ps. 133:1

Treasure your family for they are a precious gift . Love among brethren enriches one's life and brings much joy.

NOVEMBER 26

Faith is the substance of things hoped for, the evidence of things not seen.
HEB. 11:1

You cannot touch faith; you cannot see it, but it is faith that illuminates our lives and gives our souls substance.

NOVEMBER 27

Yes, I am not alone, because the Father is with me.
     JOHN 16:32

The life that is lived unto God knows divine fellowship. There is no place for loneliness for he who knows that God is with him at all times, loving and caring.

NOVEMBER 28

Unto them that are defiled and unbelieving is nothing pure; but even their mind and conscience is defiled.
     TITUS 1:15

There are among us those who, for money, pretend to be messengers of the Lord, but they are wicked and preach the gospel for personal profit. Take care in choosing a teacher.

NOVEMBER 29

And Isaac went out to meditate in the field at eventide.
GEN. 24:63

In the harried rush of modern life we must find time alone in quiet waiting upon God to affirm our belief and pledge our faithfulness.

NOVEMBER 30

Rejoice in the Lord always: and again I say, Rejoice.
PHIL. 4:4

Faith in the Lord brings joy to the soul, glory in your belief, and the glow of contentment that comes from faith.

❧ ❧ ❧

DECEMBER 1

Whosoever shall do the will of my Father which is in heaven, the same is my brother, and sister and mother.
> JESUS
> MATT. 12:50

To obey the will of God and to live by His rules is to become as kin to Jesus and to feel His presence at all times.

DECEMBER 2

Fear not them which kill the body, but are not able to kill the soul.
> JESUS
> MATT. 10:28

It is our soul which is eternal, and although our body may be harmed, if our faith remains strong, we are not hurt but can still gain eternal life.

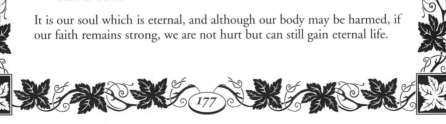

DECEMBER 3

In his disease he sought not to the Lord, but to the physician.
   2 CHRON. 16:12

The physician alone cannot heal the body. Prayer and faith will be the potion that makes his medicines effective.

DECEMBER 4

It is good and comely for one to eat and to drink and to enjoy the good of all his labour.
   ECCL. 5:18

Life is a rich feast, and because we live in a righteous manner, we enjoy the many delightful pleasures it offers.

DECEMBER 5

Scorners delight in their scorning, and fools hate knowledge.
   PROV. 1:22

Mock not that which you do not know, for when you state an opinion based on ignorance, you are seen as a fool.

DECEMBER 6

The Lord is my helper, and I will not fear what man shall do unto me.
   HEB. 13:6

With Faith in the Lord, no man can harm you, for He will shelter and care for you.

DECEMBER 7

Where two or three are gathered together in my name, there am I in the midst of them.

JESUS

MATT. 18:20

When we gather together to worship Jesus, we are not alone, for He is there in His Spirit bringing balm and peace to our souls though we may be small in number.

DECEMBER 8

If we walk in the light as He is in the light, we have fellowship one with another.

1 JOHN 1:7

Your fellow man is your brother, for we are one body in Christ and everyone members one of another. We must remember to stay in God's word.

DECEMBER 9

Shun profane and vain babblings for they will increase unto more ungodliness.
2 TIM. 2:15

We are surrounded by the noisy prattlings of fools in our media, but close your ears to them . They corrupt the spirit and cheapen the mind.

DECEMBER 10

Give us this day our daily bread.
JESUS
MATT. 6:11

If your stomach be full, mind that your soul be nourished through faith and prayer daily.

DECEMBER 11

He that walketh with wise men shall be wise; but a companion of fools shall be destroyed.
PROV. 13:20

Choose your friends carefully. One can learn much from wise companions, but the behavior of fools is contagious and their company can be degrading.

DECEMBER 12

Whosoever shall smite thee on thy right cheek, turn to him the other also.
JESUS
MATT. 5:39

Seek not revenge when you are hurt. Rather, show compassion for the anger in your enemy and treat him with kindness.

DECEMBER 13

Thou shall neither vex a stranger, nor oppress him: for ye were strangers in the land of Egypt.
    Ex. 22:21

Let us be kind to those from other lands who come amongst us. Once our people were strangers in a new land and grateful for kind behavior from those who received us.

DECEMBER 14

Hear Thou in heaven, Thy dwelling place and when Thou hearest, forgive.
    1 KINGS 8:30

If we transgress, we must pray for forgiveness. He is merciful and attentive to our prayers, and with faith and prayer we may earn His blessings.

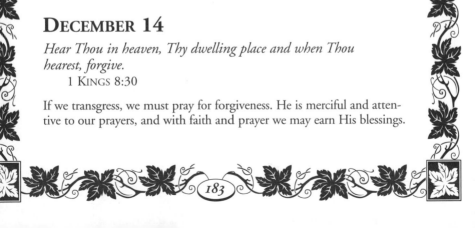

DECEMBER 15

Ye shall know the truth, and the truth shall make you free.
> JESUS
> JOHN 8:32

Through His word we know the real meaning of our lives, and through understanding we are freed from oppression and become free.

DECEMBER 16

Take no thought for the morrow: for the morrow shall take thought for the things of itself.
> JESUS
> MATT. 6:34

Do not waste your emotional strength in needless worry about what is to come; what will be will be, and today is to be lived fully without concern for the next day.

DECEMBER 17

God is my strength and power: and He maketh my way perfect.
  2 SAM. 22:23

God is with you in your every endeavor, and from Him you draw strength and power and fortitude to face the obstacles that may be in your path.

DECEMBER 18

He that saith he is in the lighty and hateth his brother, is in darkness even until now.
  1 JOHN 2:9

If you scorn your fellow man and treat him badly, you shall be alone in times of trouble with none to help or comfort you.

DECEMBER 19

It is more blessed to give than to receive.
JESUS
ACTS 20:35

He who is generous in giving will reap a rich reward, for in the giving, his spirit will grow and flourish and blessings will be bestowed upon him. For when God pays you back, it is more than you can give.

DECEMBER 20

Rejoice not when thine enemy falleth, and let not thine heart be glad when he stumbleth.
PROV. 24:17

There is no glory in revenge and no happiness to you in the besting of an enemy. Let compassion rule your heart and be not joyous at his defeat.

DECEMBER 21

The Lord is our judge, the Lord is our lawgiver, the Lord is our King. He will save us.
ISA. 33:22

The Lord is all-powerful, all-knowing. Trust in the Lord, for his eternal might surpasses all things of this world.

DECEMBER 22

Follow after righteousness, godliness, faith, love, patience, meekness.
1 TIM. 6:11

It is for the way in which we live our lives that we receive our rewards. Follow the road pointed out by Jesus Christ and you will be on the path to Heaven.

DECEMBER 23

God is not the God of the dead but of the living.
JESUS
MATT. 6:9-10

God is with us in our daily life. He is all powerful and all-knowing, and He is there with us in our every deed.

DECEMBER 24

Whatsoever ye shall ask in my name, that will I do, that the Father may be glorified in His Son.
JESUS
JOHN 14:13

The love of Jesus shines upon us, serving the glory of God. Love Him by following His word and you, too, shall glorify God.

DECEMBER 25

Grace be with all them that love our Lord Jesus Christ in sincerity.
  EPH. 6:24

On this holy day of His birth, let your mind and heart be filled with love for the birth of our savior, Jesus Christ.

DECEMBER 26

The Lord our God is righteous in all His works which he doeth.
  DAN. 1:14

Let the Lord our God be your guide, for if you are righteous in all your deeds, you shall receive His bountiful blessings.

DECEMBER 27

Thou, O Lord, art a God full of compassion, and gracious, long suffering and plenteous in mercy and truth.
    Ps. 86:15

The Lord looks upon us kindly and forgives our transgressions if we repent, for He is compassionate and merciful.

DECEMBER 28

The Lord Jesus shall be revealed from Heaven with His mighty angels, In flaming fire taking vengeance on them that know not God, and that obey not the gospel.
    2 Thess. 1:7-8

Do not let your faith waver nor your behavior deviate from that propounded by the gospels. Through the gravest troubles, hold on to your faith, for without it you are as nothing.

DECEMBER 29

If a man say, I love God, and hateth his brother, he is a liar.
    1 JOHN 4:20

To love God is to love your fellow man and to deal with him honorably. In that way, we honor God's will.

DECEMBER 30

I am thy God; I will strengthen thee; yea, I will help thee; yea, I will uphold thee with the right hand of My righteousness.
    ISA. 41:10

He is always there with you. Believe in Him, pray to Him, and His strength will give you strength in times of adversity.

DECEMBER 31

I neither received it of man, neither was I taught it, but by the revelation of Jesus Christ.
GAL. 1:12

Trust in the leading of the Holy Spirit, for he knows the truth and has set it before our eyes so that we may follow in the path of Jesus and live a life of righteousness.

❧ ❧ ❧